AF270655

TURNING INTO A DRAGONFLY

by Tyler Gieseke

Cody Koala

An Imprint of Pop!
popbooksonline.com

abdobooks.com
Published by Pop!, a division of ABDO, PO Box 398166, Minneapolis, Minnesota 55439. Copyright ©2022 by Abdo Consulting Group, Inc. International copyrights reserved in all countries. No part of this book may be reproduced in any form without written permission from the publisher. Cody Koala™ is a trademark and logo of Pop!.

Printed in the United States of America, North Mankato, Minnesota

102021
012022

THIS BOOK CONTAINS
RECYCLED MATERIALS

Cover Photo: iStockphoto
Interior Photos: Shutterstock Images, 1–13, 17–21; WildPictures / Alamy Stock Photo, 14

Editor: Elizabeth Andrews
Series Designers: Laura Graphenteen, Victoria Bates

Library of Congress Control Number: 2021942248
Publisher's Cataloging-in-Publication Data
Names: Gieseke, Tyler, author.
Title: Turning into a dragonfly / by Tyler Gieseke
Description: Minneapolis, Minnesota : Pop!, 2022 | Series: Transforming animals | Includes online resources and index.
Identifiers: ISBN 9781098241155 (lib. bdg.) | ISBN 9781098241858 (ebook)
Subjects: LCSH: Dragonflies--Juvenile literature. | Insects--Juvenile literature. | Animal life cycles--Juvenile literature. | Insects--Metamorphosis--Juvenile literature. | Animal Behavior--Juvenile literature.
Classification: DDC 595.7--dc23

Hello! My name is

Cody Koala

Pop open this book and you'll find QR codes like this one, loaded with information, so you can learn even more!

Scan this code* and others like it while you read, or visit the website below to make this book pop.

popbooksonline.com/turn-dragonfly

*Scanning QR codes requires a web-enabled smart device with a QR code reader app and a camera.

Table of Contents

Chapter 1

Transforming Animals

Dragonflies dart around rivers and lakes. They are brightly colored bugs. They live all over the world. Many people think they are beautiful.

Watch a video here!

Life Cycle of a Dragonfly

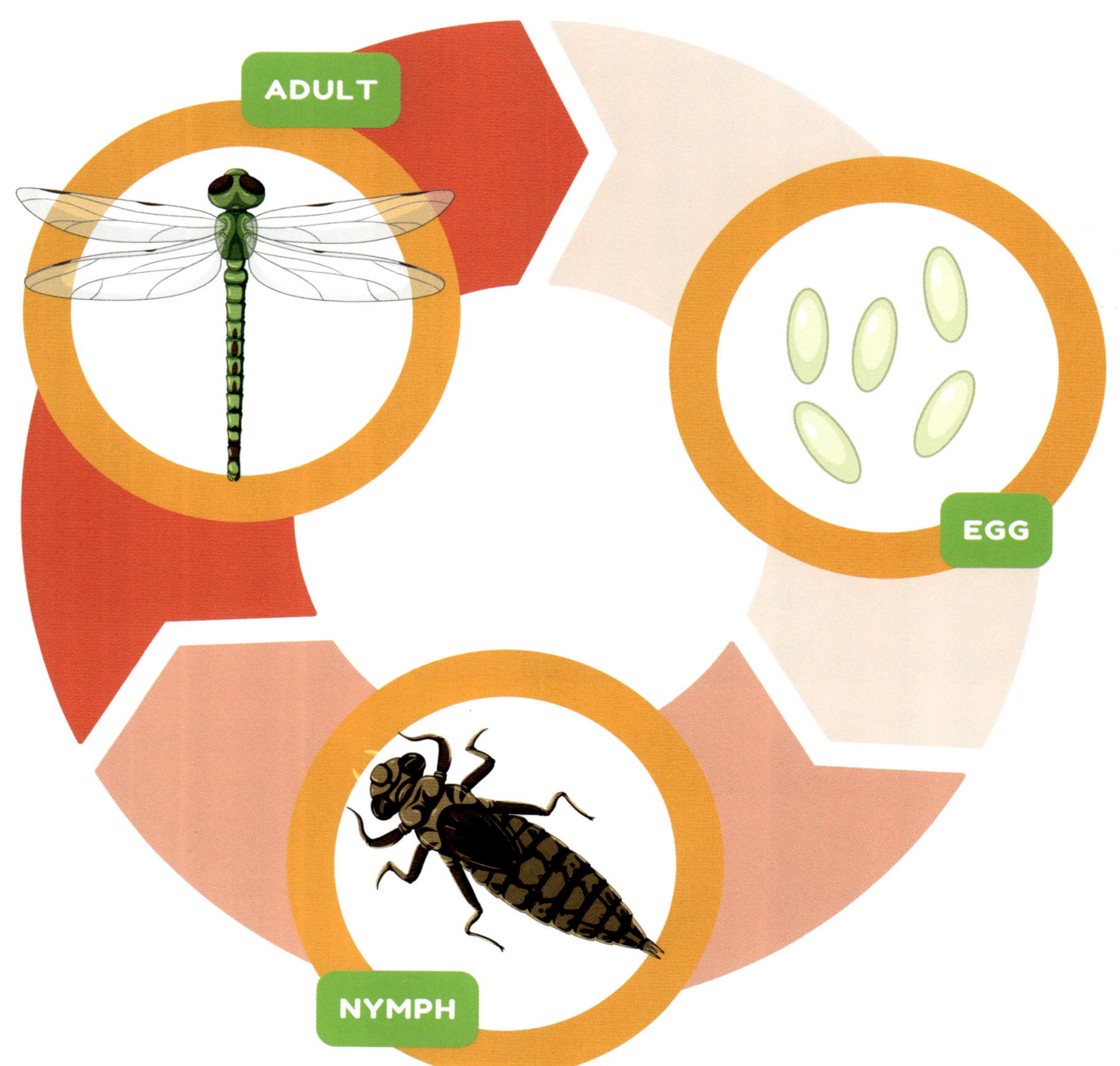

Dragonflies are **transforming** animals. They grow through the dragonfly life cycle. Its three steps are egg, nymph, and adult.

Adult dragonflies have four wings. They have six legs and two eyes.

Chapter 2

Dragonfly Eggs

Dragonflies start life as eggs. Female dragonflies put their eggs in the water. Some put them in plant stems or wood.

Dragonflies have been on Earth for at least 300 million years.

Learn more here!

adult
eggs

Female dragonflies can lay hundreds of eggs. The eggs are small and round. The eggs **hatch** after a few weeks. Then, the next step of the cycle begins!

Chapter 3

Life as a Nymph

Dragonflies are called nymphs when they **hatch**. They live underwater and breathe using **gills**. Nymphs are usually a dull color. They are only a few inches long.

Complete an
activity here!

Nymphs are **predators**. They hunt and eat small water animals. These include **tadpoles** and small fish.

Nymphs have a hard shell that covers their bodies. They **molt** this shell as they grow. Nymphs molt between five and 14 times. This takes a few years.

Chapter 4

Taking Flight

A nymph becomes an adult dragonfly during its final **molt**. This happens above the water. It is called emergence.

Learn more here!

Emergence takes about
12 hours from start to end.

The nymph grips a plant stem. Then it breaks out of its old shell. The dragonfly waits for its new shell to dry. Its wings unfold for the first time!

Adult dragonflies fly away from water to find food. They eat other insects. Then they return to the water to **mate**.

An adult dragonfly
lives for only one to six
weeks. During this time,
females lay their eggs.
The life cycle starts again!
Dragonflies are amazing
transforming animals.

Making Connections

Text-to-Self

Which is your favorite step in the dragonfly life cycle? Why?

Text-to-Text

Have you read other books about bugs? How are those bugs similar to dragonflies? How are they different?

Text-to-World

What is another transforming animal you know about? How is its life cycle similar to or different from a dragonfly's?

Glossary

gills – body parts that help animals breathe water.

hatch – to break out of an egg.

mate – to create new eggs or babies with a partner.

molt – to shed.

predator – an animal that hunts other animals for food.

tadpole – the name for some small water animals before they become adults.

transform – to change into a new shape.

Index